Mapping Our World

Sandy Phan

Consultants

Shelley Scudder
Gifted Education Teacher
Broward County Schools

Caryn Williams, M.S.Ed.
Madison County Schools
Huntsville, AL

Publishing Credits

Conni Medina, M.A.Ed., *Managing Editor*
Lee Aucoin, *Creative Director*
Torrey Maloof, *Editor*
Marissa Rodriguez, *Designer*
Stephanie Reid, *Photo Editor*
Rachelle Cracchiolo, M.S.Ed., *Publisher*

Image Credits: p. 2–3, 28–29 Alamy; p. 24–25 Getty Images; p. 29(top) iStockphoto; p. 7, 10 Mapping Specialists; p. 4 dpa/picture-alliance/Newscom; p. 9 Newscom; p. 13 ZUMA Press/Newscom; All other images Shutterstock.

Teacher Created Materials
5301 Oceanus Drive
Huntington Beach, CA 92649-1030
http://www.tcmpub.com

ISBN 978-1-4333-7000-7

Printed by: 51497
Printed in: China

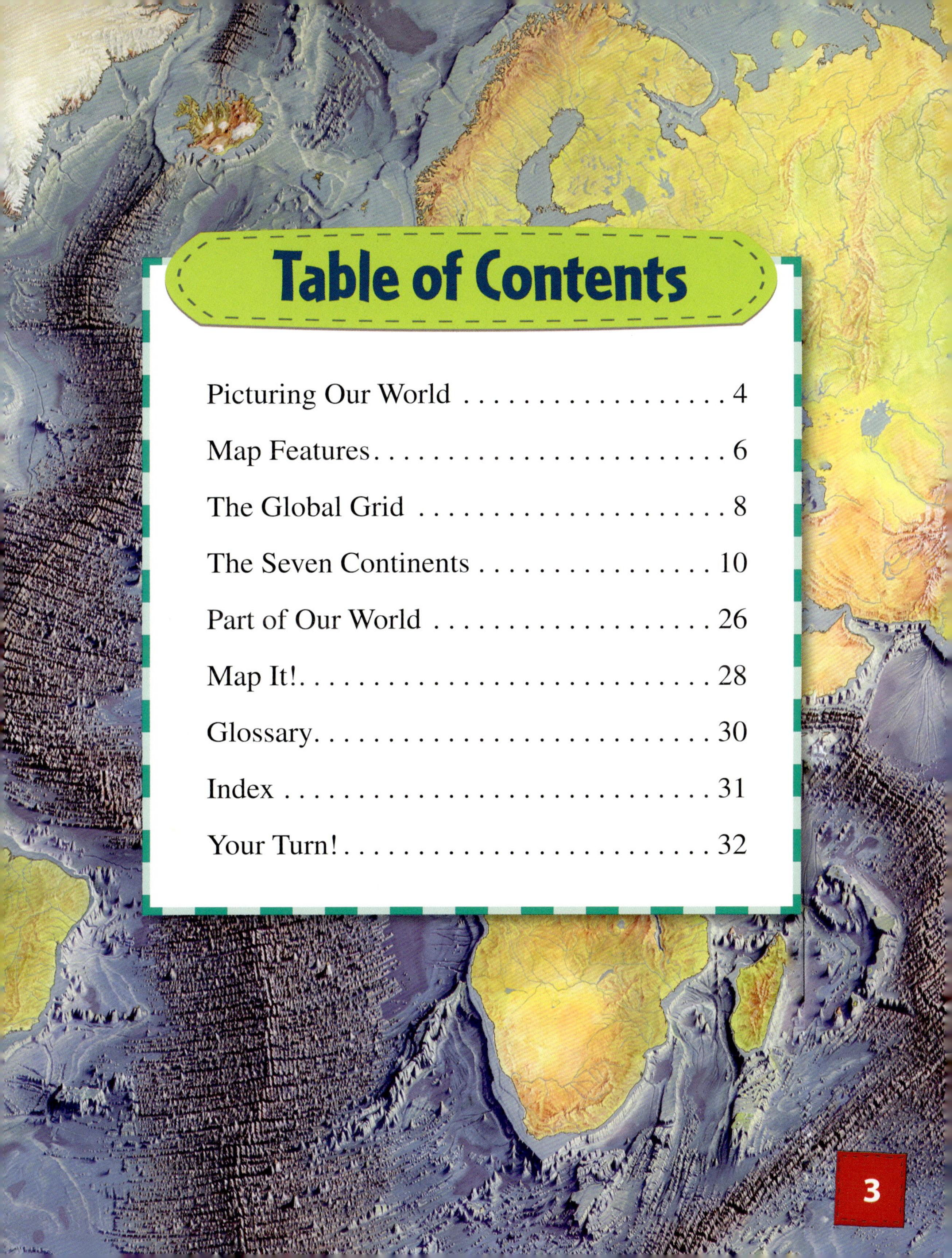

Table of Contents

This old map was drawn on clay.

Picturing Our World

Maps help us know where we are. They show how Earth's land, water, and places come together. Long ago, people drew maps on clay, bark, and animal skins. They used maps to get around and to find food and water.

These students are using a globe.

Today, we can look at a globe. This is a model of Earth. We also have flat maps. There are even electronic (ih-lek-TRON-ik) maps. All these different kinds of maps help us see our world.

Map Features

A map is a small picture of a large area. Maps have many features. A compass rose shows four directions: north, south, east, and west. Some maps only have an arrow that points north. Some maps have scales. Scales show what a length on a map equals in real distance.

This is a compass rose.

Maps also have legends, sometimes called *keys*. A legend tells you what the symbols, lines, and colors on a map mean. Knowing these features can help you read and better understand maps.

This map has a scale, a legend, and a compass rose.

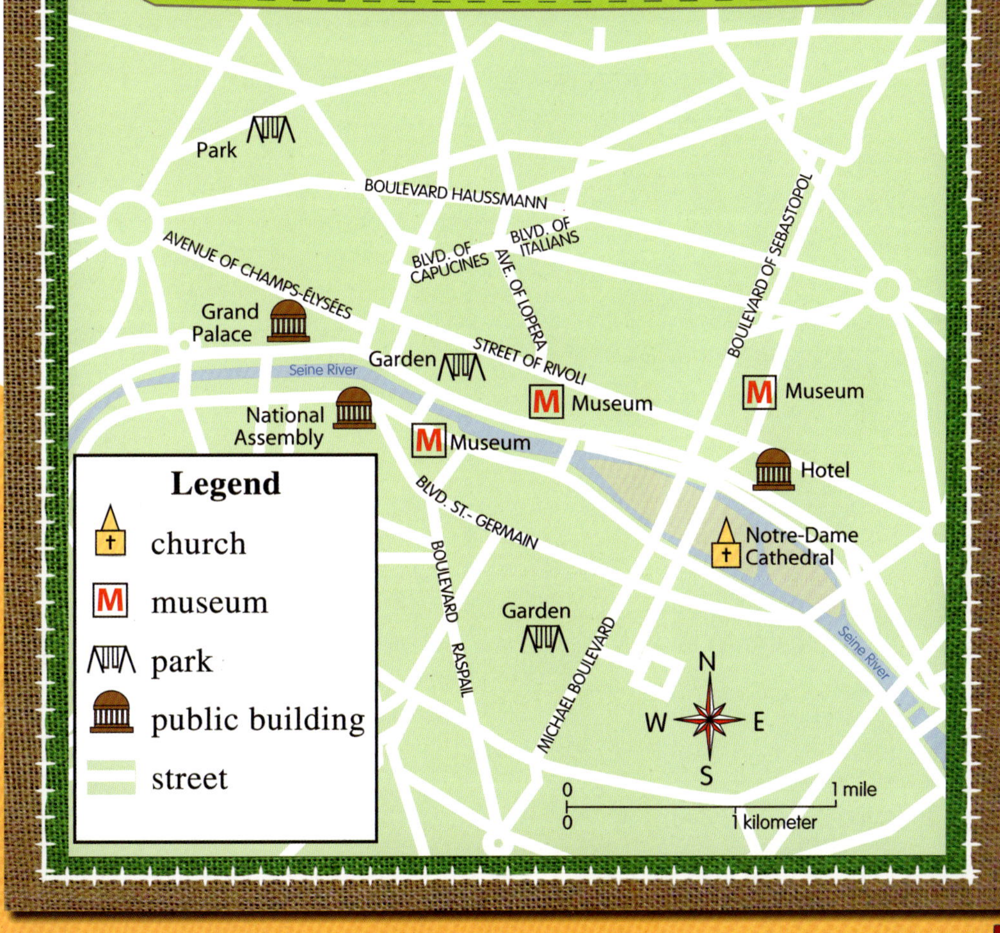

The Global Grid

The global grid is a set of imaginary lines on a map. These lines help us find places on Earth's surface.

Lines of **latitude** (LAT-i-tood) run east and west. Lines of **longitude** (LON-ji-tood) run north and south.

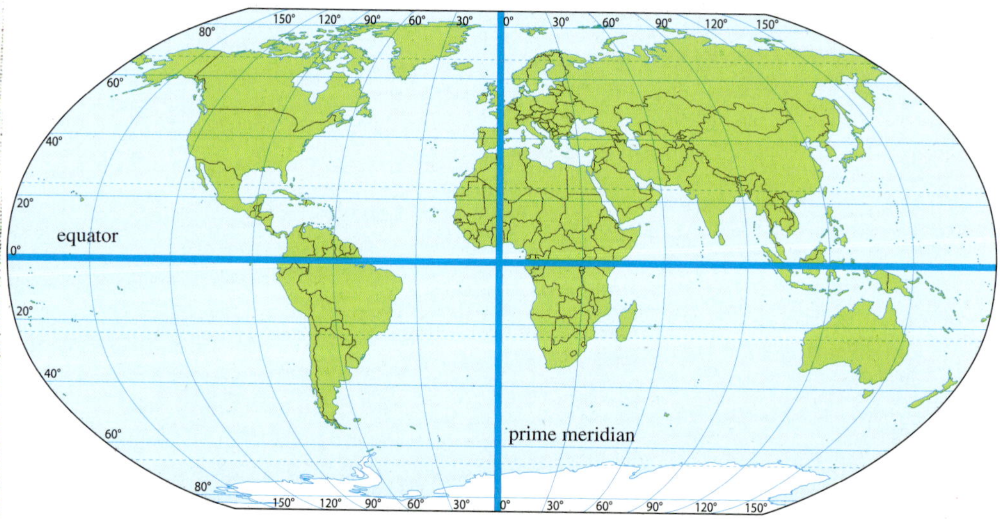

This map shows the prime meridian and the equator.

The **equator** (ih-KWEY-ter) is a line of latitude. It is in the exact middle of Earth. The **prime meridian** is a line of longitude. The prime meridian and the equator are the starting points for the global grid.

This man is using the global grid to find a place on Earth.

The Seven Continents

Physical maps show how nature shapes the world. They show landforms such as mountains, valleys, and plains. **Political maps** show borders between places. They show how people have split up the land.

Elevation

Elevation (el-uh-VEY-shuhn) can also be shown on physical maps. Elevation is the height of a place.

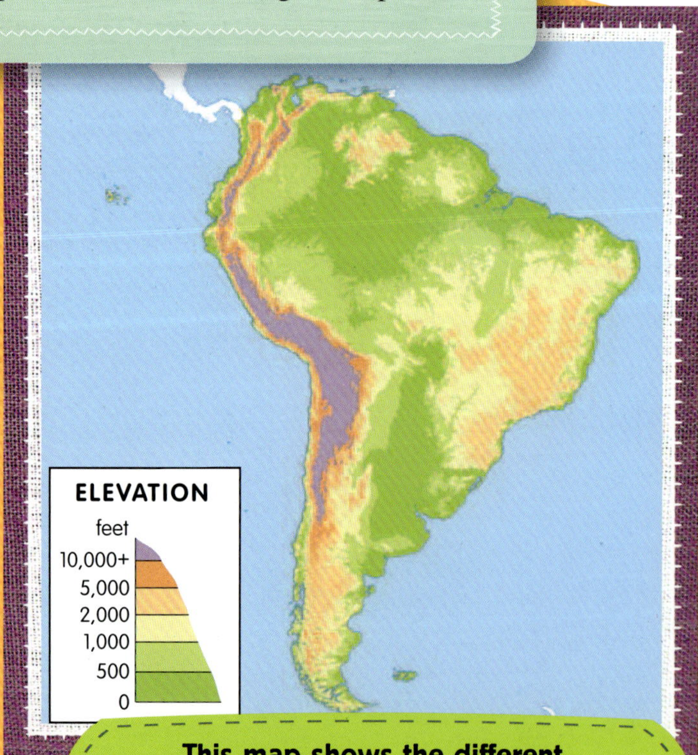

This map shows the different elevations of South America.

Water covers two-thirds of Earth's surface. Most of this water is in the ocean. Water can also be found in lakes, rivers, and streams. Seven **continents**, or landmasses, make up the rest of Earth's surface.

This map shows the seven continents.

Asia

Asia (EY-shuh) is the largest continent on Earth. More than half of the world's people live in Asia. Most of these people live in China and India.

One Big Country

Russia is the largest country in the world. It stretches across two continents: Europe (YOOR-uhp) and Asia!

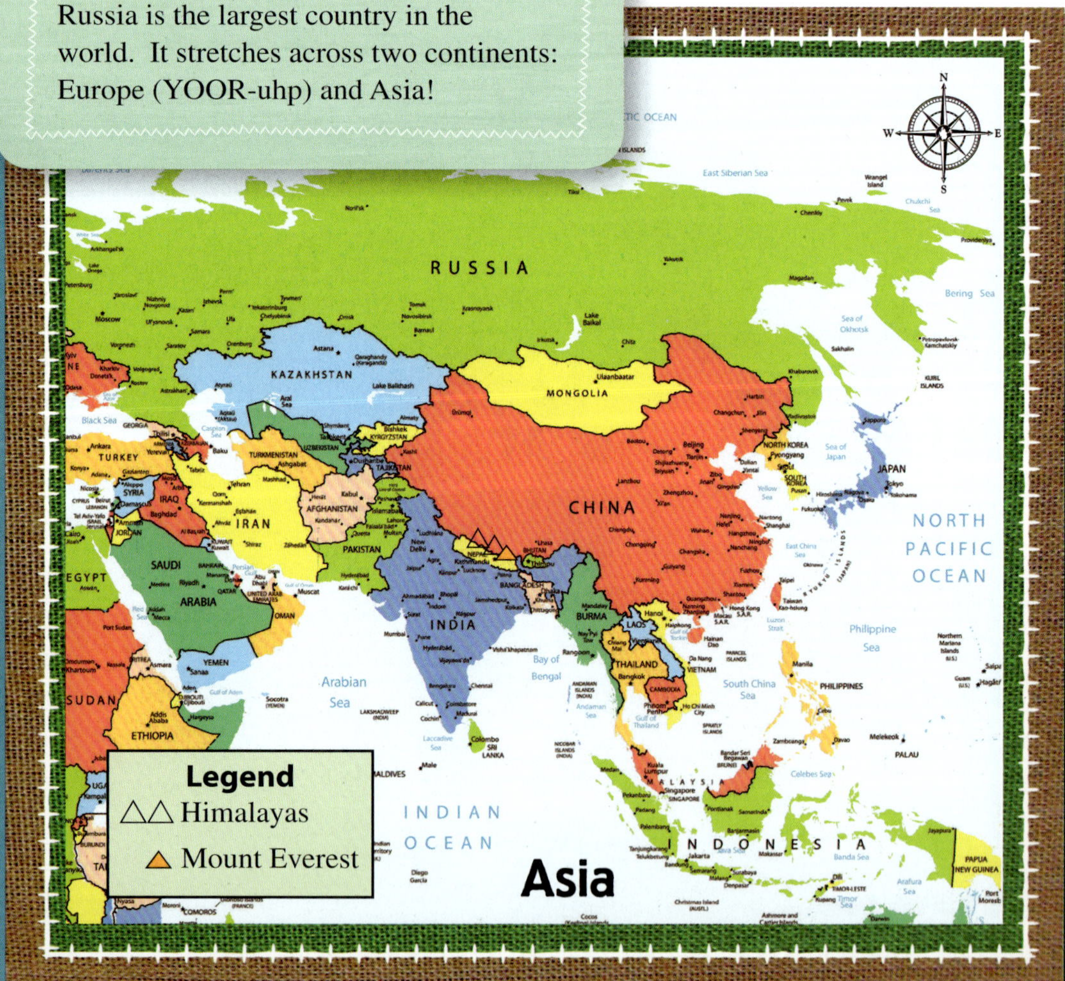

Asia is home to the Himalaya (him-uh-LEY-uh) Mountains. The mountains have over 100 peaks. Mount Everest is one of them. It is the tallest mountain in the world.

Asia is also home to the lowest point on Earth, the Dead Sea. It lies between Israel (IZ-ree-uhl) and Jordan. If you swim in the Dead Sea, you will float easily! This is because there is so much salt in the water.

Some people climb to the top of Mount Everest.

Africa

Africa is the second-largest continent. The Sahara desert takes up almost all of the northern half of the continent. It is the largest desert in the world. The Nile River runs north through Africa. It is the longest river in the world! In northern Egypt, you will find the famous pyramids of Giza (GEE-zuh).

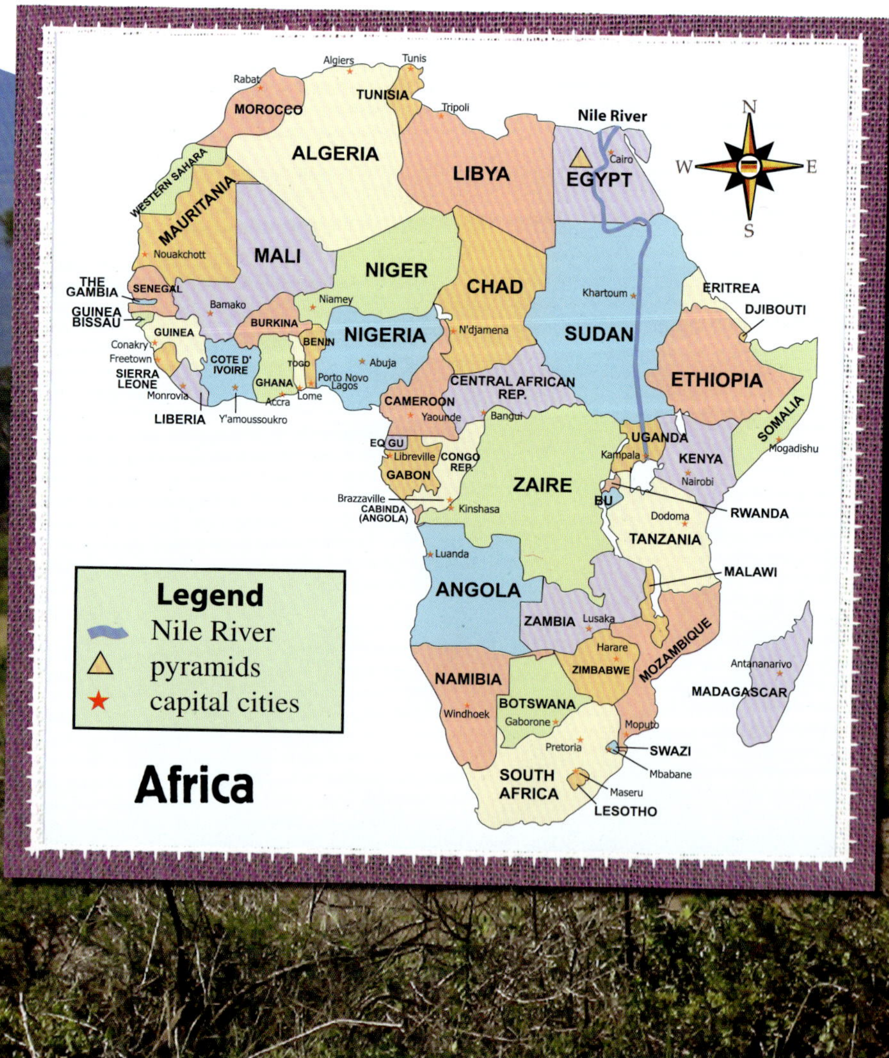

Africa is also home to many animals. The country of Tanzania (tan-zuh-NEE-uh) has a lot of wildlife. It is home to hippos and giraffes. There are also lions and leopards. Elephants and zebras roam the land, too!

This is an African elephant.

North America

North America is the third-largest continent in the world. The highest point on this continent is Mount McKinley. It is in Alaska. The lowest point is Death Valley. It is in California. North America is made of some of the oldest rocks in the world! These rocks are called the Canadian Shield.

The Rocky Mountains run through much of North America.

Natural resources (REE-sohrs-ez) come from nature. They are items such as wood, soil, and oil. They are used to make other things. North America has many natural resources. It has large forests and rich soil. Resources like these help the countries in North America make money.

South America

South America is another continent. Most of South America has a **tropical** climate. That means it is warm almost all the time. The Andes Mountains are in South America. They make up the longest mountain range in the world! They run the whole length of the continent.

The Amazon River is also in South America. More water flows through this river than any other river in the world. The Amazon Rainforest is in South America, too. It is the world's largest tropical rainforest. It is home to millions of plants, animals, and insects. There are so many that people are still finding new ones!

Save the Rainforest

People have been chopping down the rainforest for years. They use the trees for wood, paper, medicines, and more. These things are important, but so are the rainforests. We need to protect them.

This is a giant centipede.

This is a waterfall in the Amazon Rainforest.

Antarctica

Antarctica is another continent. Ice sheets cover most of Antarctica. Ice sheets are very large and thick areas of ice. The South Pole lies at the center of the continent. The coldest temperature ever recorded on Earth was recorded here. It was -76°F (-60°C). That is more than 100 degrees below freezing!

What About People?

There are about 4,000 humans living on Antarctica. They are mostly scientists. They study the land, ocean, and animals.

These are penguins in Antarctica.

Although it is very cold in Antarctica, plants and animals do live on or near the continent. There are 45 types of birds. This includes penguins. Whales and seals also live in the waters around the continent.

Europe

The continent of Europe has many islands and **peninsulas**. Peninsulas are landforms that have water on three sides. This means that most places in Europe are close to water.

Europe is home to many famous cities. You can visit London, England, and see the Tower Bridge. It was built in 1894 on the Thames (TEMZ) River. It is one of the most famous bridges in the world. Or you can visit Paris, France, and see the Eiffel (AHY-fuhl) Tower. It was built in 1889. Many of the cities in Europe are old and have many stories to tell!

This is the Tower Bridge in London, England.

This is Paris, France.

Australia

Australia (aw-STREYL-yuh) is the smallest continent. It is the only continent that is just one country. Much of Australia has an arid climate. This means that it does not rain much. It is mostly hot.

the Great Barrier Reef

Many people visit Australia. Some go to see the Great Barrier Reef. It is made up of the largest amount of coral in the world. There are at least 300 kinds of coral in the reef. Australia is also known for its unique animals. There are kangaroos, koalas (koh-AH-luhz), and kookaburras (KOOK-uh-bur-uhz)!

Summer Holiday

Australia is in the southern hemisphere. This means that it is south of the equator. Because of this, Australia's winter months are June through August. Its summer is December through February. So, Australia's Christmas takes place in the summer!

These koalas are sleeping.

Part of Our World

Maps remind us how large our world is. Maps show us all the different countries and landforms. They help us understand the climates and resources. Maps point out how places and people work together. They show us how people and nature shape our world.

This girl uses a globe to explore the world.

Maps let us explore our world. They can help us find our way. Mapping our world helps us better understand Earth and one another.

This boy uses a map to find a campsite.

Map It!

Use your imagination! Think of a new continent. Make a map of this place. Be sure to include landforms and a legend. Talk about your map with a friend or a family member.

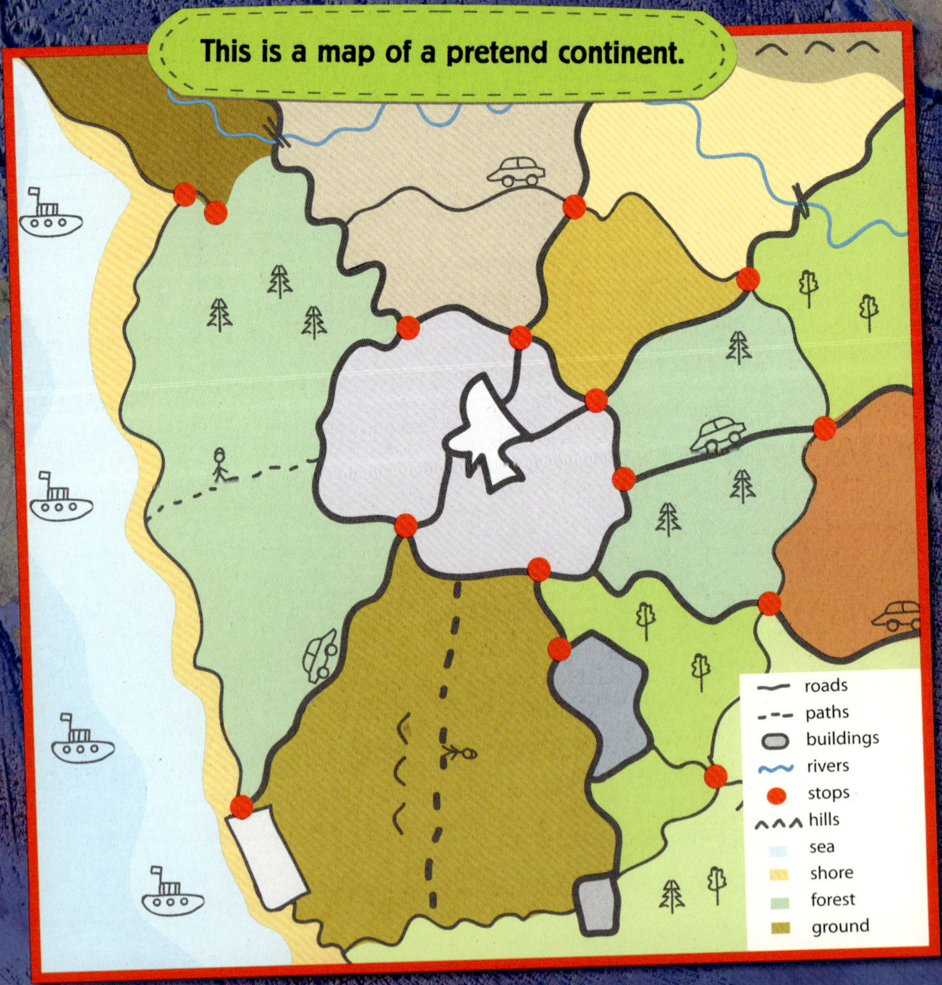

This girl is imagining a new continent.

- roads
- paths
- buildings
- rivers
- stops
- hills
- sea
- shore
- forest
- ground

This is the legend for the map.

Glossary

continents—the seven great landmasses on Earth

equator—the line of latitude that is the same distance from the North Pole and the South Pole

latitude—imaginary lines that run east and west around Earth

longitude—imaginary lines that run from the North Pole to the South Pole

natural resources—materials found in nature such as water or wood

peninsulas—areas of land that are surrounded by water on three sides

physical maps—maps that show a place's land and water

political maps—maps that show how people have split up the land

prime meridian—the line of longitude that runs from the North Pole to the South Pole and passes through Greenwich, England

tropical—relating to the part of the world near the equator where the weather is very warm

Index

Your Turn!

Pack Your Bags

These kids are using a globe to find continents. They can find places they have never visited.

After reading this book, which continent would you most like to visit? Why? Write a list of what you would pack to take on a trip to that continent.